IMAGES
of America

BOSTON COMMON

The Brewer Fountain was photographed about 1930. (Courtesy BPL, Leslie Jones Collection.)

IMAGES
of America

BOSTON COMMON

Friends of the Public Garden

ARCADIA
PUBLISHING

Copyright © 2005 by Friends of the Public Garden
ISBN 9781531623135

Published by Arcadia Publishing
Charleston, South Carolina

Library of Congress Catalog Card Number: 2005927375

For all general information contact Arcadia Publishing at:
Telephone 843-853-2070
Fax 843-853-0044
E-mail sales@arcadiapublishing.com
For customer service and orders:
Toll-Free 1-888-313-2665

Visit us on the Internet at www.arcadiapublishing.com

CONTENTS

ACKNOWLEDGMENTS

We acknowledge with great appreciation the assistance of the following: Jackie Donovan of the American Antiquarian Society; Pat Boulos, Sally Pierce, and Catharina Slatterback of the Boston Athenaeum; Kathleen Cable of the *Boston Globe*; Alan Thibault of the *Boston Herald*; Katherine Higgins of the Boston Parks and Recreation Department; Boston Photo Imaging; Aaron Schmidt of the Boston Public Library; Lauren Mandel and Holly Smith of the Bostonian Society; Lorna Conlon, Sally Hinkle, and Emily Novak of Historic New England/SPNEA; Kimberly Nusco and Anne E. Bentley of the Massachusetts Historical Society; Eugenie Beal; James Faulk; Helen Hannon; Ellen Kolemainen; Fred Mauet; Barbara W. Moore; Anne Swanson; and Thomas E. Weesner.

Our thanks also go to Linda MacIver at the Boston Public Library for research assistance; Constance G. Schnitger for map work; Michael C. Stone, DDS, for access to his extensive photograph collection; and Maureen A. Taylor for assistance in dating and interpreting the photographs. Information on Father Leonard Feeney was drawn from John Deedy's *American Catholicism—and Now Where*, published by Plenum Press, New York and London, in 1987.

Photographs provided by the Boston Public Library Print Department are credited to BPL. Those owned by the Friends of the Public Garden are identified as FPG.

The Friends of the Public Garden is a nonprofit advocacy group founded in 1970 to preserve and enhance the Garden and the neighboring Common. The Friends number more than 2,500 members and many volunteers. For information on membership and current activities, visit our Web site at friendsofthepublicgarden.org or contact:

Friends of the Public Garden
87 Mount Vernon Street
Boston, Massachusetts 02108
617-723-8144
fopg@gis.net

This book was prepared by a committee of several friends of the Public Garden: Linda Cox, Henry Lee, Margo Miller, and Gail Weesner.

INTRODUCTION

The Common has belonged to the people of Boston since 1634, just four years after the town's establishment. Occupied for millennia by Native Americans, the narrow and hilly peninsula called Shawmut had in 1630 but one resident—an Anglican clergyman named William Blackstone. The Puritans of the Massachusetts Bay Colony had first settled in nearby Charlestown, but learning of ample water sources on Shawmut and invited by Blackstone, they moved across the river to a new home, which they promptly renamed Boston after the Lincolnshire town where some of them had lived and worshiped. The colonists granted Blackstone his farm, today the Common and part of Beacon Hill, and by formal agreement acquired rights to all the peninsula from the Algonquin sachem, Chichatabut.

In 1634, when Blackstone decided to leave for Rhode Island, the town purchased 50 acres of his open land for £30, for which it assessed each household no less than six shillings. In English custom, the colonists set aside the field for common use, in particular military training and the grazing of cattle. In 1640, to prevent the Common's division, it was ordered that "henceforth there shall be no land granted eyther for houseplot or garden to any person out of the open ground or Common field." Six years later, it was voted that "noe common marish and pastur Ground shall hereafter by gifts or sayle, exchange or otherwise, be counted unto property without consent of ye major part of ye inhabitants of ye towne." This commitment, confirmed in the City Charter of 1822, protects the Common to the present day from sale in part or whole.

The Common is described in the 17th century as rolling scrubland with four hills and three ponds, extending to the marshes of the Charles River estuary, now the site of the Public Garden. Like the rest of the peninsula, it had few trees, though one, the Great Elm, stood in proud eminence until 1876. While only one hill and one pond remain and trees now abound, the Common today is nearly the same size and configuration as in 1634, a relic of an ancient landscape where one may truly walk in the steps of the Puritan founders and all who followed.

By early law, each household could graze one cow or four sheep with a limit of 70 cows (and one horse belonging to Elder Oliver). Cows and militia went easily together, with the exception of Gen. Humphrey Atherton who, riding across the Common one evening in 1661, struck a cow and was killed. Along Tremont Street stood a tree-lined mall where "gentlemen and ladies" would promenade at teatime, though never on Sunday. From earliest times, the Common was a center of community life, a place of execution and punishment, public sermons (several by the famed evangelist George Whitefield), annual processions of North and South Enders on Guy Fawkes Day, a show of 300 women spinning, the roasting of a whole ox, and grand celebrations like that in 1766 marking repeal of the Stamp Act with an obelisk alight with 280 lanterns, fireworks, and a pipe of Madeira donated by John Hancock.

Throughout the Colonial years, the Common was a focal point of military activity, a drill ground for militia, a gathering place for expeditionary forces, and, for eight years before March 1776, a military encampment and fortification. From its shore, Redcoats departed on April 18, 1775, for Lexington and Concord, and here they buried their dead following the Battle of Bunker

Hill. Entering the evacuated town a year later, George Washington inspected the Common, badly battered but reclaimed and forever after a source of civic pride.

With construction of the Massachusetts State House in 1797, new residences, many the work of Charles Bulfinch, arose along Tremont, Park, and Beacon Streets. Reflecting its surroundings, the Common gradually became more park than pasture. By 1830, the city had banished the cows, filled several ponds, and added tree-lined malls and paths, and in 1836, the whole was encircled with handsome iron fencing. Where scarcely a tree had stood, there were by 1851 some 1,255, largely elms and evergreens. The popular Wishing Stone near Beacon Street disappeared, but the Frog Pond, enhanced in time by granite curbing and a giant waterspout, remained a central feature of the park.

Viewing the Common in 1840, Nathaniel Hawthorne confided to his notebook, "Blessed be God for this green tract and the view which it affords." William Makepeace Thackeray, visiting Boston a decade later, pronounced the elms along Beacon Street in a class with those at Windsor Castle.

More than ever, the Common was host to speeches and exhibitions of every nature, including an appearance by Amelia Bloomer, temperance and women's rights reformer, in the costume of skirt and Turkish pants that would bear her name. Militias in great number continued to parade, often before noted visitors: Washington in 1789, President Monroe in 1817, Lafayette on his famed tour in 1824, President Jackson and most of his cabinet in 1833, Hungarian hero Louis Kossuth in 1851, and the Prince of Wales, future Edward VII, in 1860.

During the Civil War, recruiting tents dotted the Common, and from its Parade Ground, Massachusetts regiments were dispatched and mustered. Here Bostonians celebrated the war's end and soon afterwards mourned the loss of their president. Postwar years brought a countless variety of events and activities—sledding and kite flying, the beginnings of football and baseball, mass meetings including a Whig Party convention, balloon ascensions, carpet beating, a showing of Lincoln's log cabin, fireworks, American Indian war dances, speeches galore, and, as always, famous visitors.

In the national enthusiasm for public art, the city soon embellished its parks and squares with sculpture. Gardner Brewer, whose house had replaced that of John Hancock, presented the Common with a fountain purchased at the Paris Exposition in 1867. Then 10 years later came Martin Milmore's monument to the soldiers and sailors of the Civil War, and in 1897, the magnificent bronze memorial to Col. Robert Gould Shaw and the 54th Regiment by Augustus Saint-Gaudens.

Throughout the 19th century, the Common stood inviolate, the mere threat of encroachment encountering fierce public opposition. Testifying with others against a proposed structure in 1877, a Catholic priest expressed a popular view by telling the aldermen, "I speak for the poor, and I say you have no right morally and before God to take away this heritage." The proposal quickly died. In 1893, a plan to relieve traffic by laying trolley tracks across the Common drew a remonstrance of 1,500 Boston women headed by Julia Ward Howe. It, too, met defeat, but a compromise solution three years later brought the nation's first subway running beneath the Common and emerging in the Public Garden. Although a wonder of its time, it foreshadowed further inflictions in years to come.

To meet new traffic woes, now from automobiles, in 1960, the state constructed the Under Common Garage, a practical but ultimately damaging public service. By the 1970s, the Common had suffered as well from many years of neglect, with half of its trees lost, the Frog Pond empty, fountains defunct, the fencing removed, and a grave imbalance of use and care. Yet, as Mark Anthony DeWolfe Howe had noted in 1910, whenever this heritage cried out to be saved, "there was an army ready to save it." In the last decades of the 20th century, public-private efforts brought notable improvements, including new fencing, a refurbished playground and bandstand, information kiosks, a rejuvenated Frog Pond with an artificial ice rink, and in the 1990s, the Common Management Plan for future maintenance and control.

In care or neglect, the Common remained through the 20th century a center stage of city life. In two world wars, it was the site of recruiting booths, troop entertainment, bond sales, and even victory gardens. Thousands cheered Charles Lindbergh in 1927 after his solo flight across the Atlantic, protested the execution of Sacco and Vanzetti and later the Vietnam War, celebrated the city's tercentennial in 1930, welcomed personages such as Martin Luther King Jr. speaking against segregation in schools and housing, and, in 1979, Pope John Paul II conducting the first papal mass in North America.

Not far from its 400th birthday, the Common today is an historic landmark redolent with memories. In equal tradition, it is a valued resource for the people of Boston and many thousands of annual visitors—a place of sports, informal and organized; exhibitions; musical events; a Shakespeare festival; rallies and protests; charity and art shows; and on New Year's Eve, Boston's famous First Night. Despite a continuing struggle with overuse and lack of funding, it is still a green retreat of lawns and venerable trees in the heart of the city. People still rest on its benches, walk their dogs, hear speakers, or watch a happy throng of skaters. Once a year in long custom, the Ancient and Honorable Artillery Company, formed in 1638, marches again before the dignitaries of the day. And perhaps, too, in the quiet of an evening, the shade of John Winthrop or young Ben Franklin still walks along familiar paths of America's oldest and most venerated green space.

William Blackstone (left) greets John Winthrop at a place on or near Boston Common in 1630. This detail is from the 1930 Founders Monument by John F. Paramino. (Photograph by Thomas E. Weesner.)

One

THE FIRST CENTURY

For more than 100 years after Boston's founding, the only historical images of the Common are written descriptions: it was almost treeless with scattered rocks and brambles; the western shore was a tidal bog; there were three ponds and three hills. If any early settlers sketched views of the Common, these have not survived, but later generations have tried to recreate its image—with maps, topographical views, and even verse.

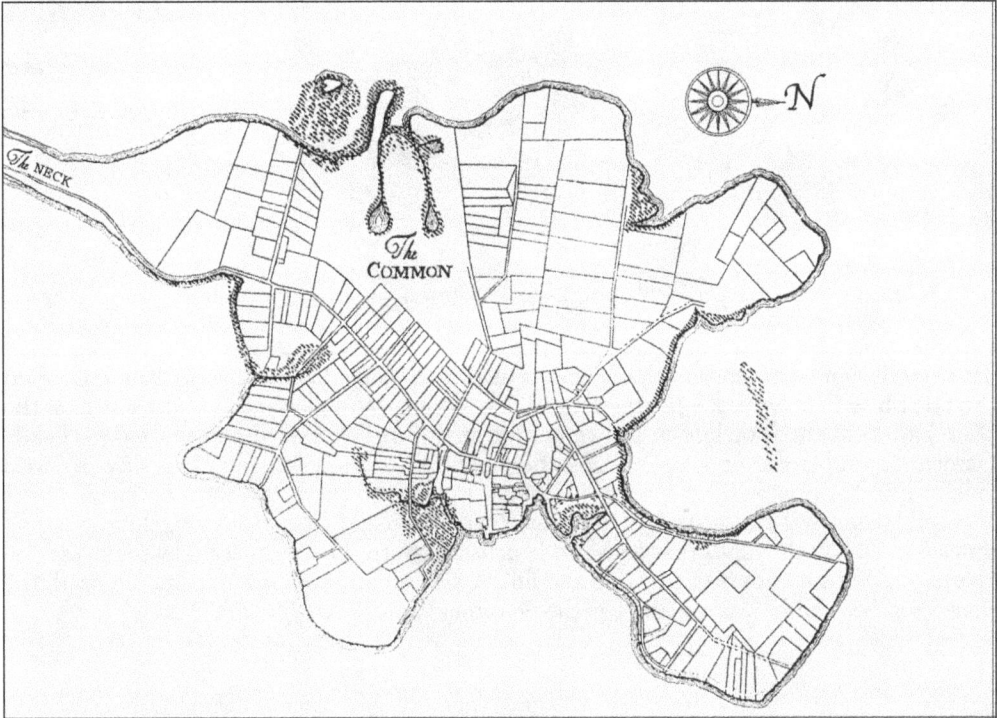

This map, adapted from one published by the Colonial Society in 1930, is based on a study of land ownership in 1643 Boston. It shows the early town with its narrow "neck" extending toward the mainland. The Common already displays its distinctive trapezoidal form. Near the soggy shoreline, three ponds drain into the Back Bay waters: Cow Pond to the south, the tiny Sheehan's Pond near the shoreline, and the surviving Frog Pond.

This sketch shows the lands of the Common as they probably looked from Beacon Hill when the English settlers arrived: a lightly wooded field sloping gently toward the tidal waters of the Back Bay. Near the shoreline in the center foreground is Fox Hill, the site of today's Public Garden; beyond is the neck connecting the peninsula to the mainland. This view is based on a c. 1935 drawing by Ethel Stanwood Bolton. In his 1859 poem "Boston Common," Oliver Wendell Holmes sets the scene: "All overgrown with brush and fern, / And straggling clumps of tangled trees, / With trunks that lean and boughs that turn, / Bent eastward by the mastering breeze, — / With spongy bogs that drip and fill / A yellow pond with muddy rain, / Beneath the shaggy southern Hill / Lies wet and low the Shawmut plain." (Courtesy FPG.)

The sole inhabitant of Boston in 1630 was William Blackstone (or Blaxton), a reclusive Church of England clergyman. The new settlers found him living in a cottage on the south slope of Beacon Hill, overlooking the rugged scrublands of the future Common. This imaginative image appeared in 1882 in James H. Stark's *Antique Views of Boston*. (Courtesy FPG.)

Along the Beacon Street Mall, opposite the foot of Spruce Street, is the 1930 Founders Monument, a large bas-relief celebrating the city's 300th birthday. It portrays Blackstone welcoming John Winthrop's Puritan band to Shawmut peninsula. The monument site was thoughtfully chosen since tradition places the encounter close to Blackstone's cottage, located near the Beacon-Spruce corner. Sculptor John F. Paramino once studied with Augustus Saint-Gaudens. (Photograph by Thomas E. Weesner.)

The most conspicuous feature on the Common was a tree. Known as the Great Elm, it was much loved by generations of Bostonians and appears often in early views. According to tradition, its limbs were used for hangings. Witches, pirates, common criminals, and religious dissenters (especially Quakers) all received harsh treatment from the Puritans here. This drawing dates from 1850. (Courtesy Bostonian Society/Old State House.)

On the east lawn of the Massachusetts State House is the seated bronze figure of Mary Dyer, a militant Quaker hanged on June 1, 1660, reportedly on the Common. The work of Sylvia Shaw Judson, the statue was erected in 1959. It is, in the words of historian Walter Muir Whitehill, "a charming idealization, considerably more peaceful than its subject was in life." (Courtesy Boston Parks and Recreation Department.)

The First Muster, an oil painting from around 1901, shows John Winthrop reviewing the Ancient and Honorable Artillery Company on the Common in 1639. The election of officers that took place at that time has been repeated every year since. (This fanciful depiction shows a heavily wooded Common; in truth, it was almost treeless.) The Ancients are the oldest military order in America and, after the London Artillery and the Swiss Guard, the third oldest in the world. (Courtesy Ancient and Honorable Artillery Company.)

The Common's South Burying Ground, established in 1756, was the fourth cemetery in Colonial Boston. British soldiers killed at Bunker Hill are said to be buried here. These grounds have been much disturbed through the years. In 1836, two rows of tombs were covered over to create the Boylston Street Mall, and the site was excavated thoroughly during subway construction in the 1890s. (Courtesy Massachusetts State House Library.)

Perhaps the best-known person buried here is the artist Gilbert Stuart, who died penniless in 1828 and was entombed in the vault of friends. The original grave site no longer exists, but a memorial plaque was installed by the Paint and Clay Club in 1897. The prominent Boston photographer Baldwin Coolidge photographed the plaque in 1912. (Courtesy Historic New England/SPNEA.)

Two

TRAINING FIELD
AND PASTURE

In the Revolutionary War era, a few contemporary images of the Common begin to be seen. Not surprisingly, some are of military origin, but others show a rural pasture already used for recreation and pleasure. The rendering of the early views is often primitive, but by 1800, they display some sophistication. Many of the images in this section originated as the work of amateurs, which later generations reproduced as lithographs or engravings.

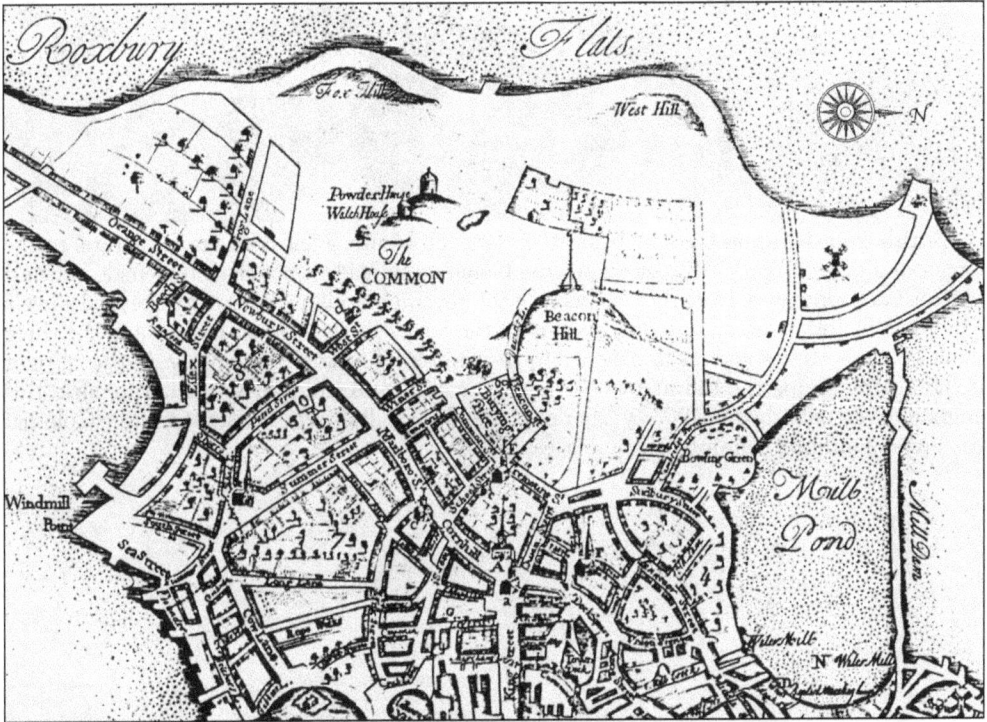

In 1728, the Common is shown as an open field with one tree, the Great Elm, and one pool of water, Frog Pond. There are two adjacent hills, Powder House (today known as Flagstaff) and Watch House (now undefined). Fox Hill, at the water's edge, was an island at high tide; it was fortified during the Revolution and then leveled to fill nearby lowlands. This map is a detail, slightly modified, of the original by William Burgis. (Courtesy FPG.)

As British troops drill on the field below the Hancock House, a few cows are at pasture. In the foreground is the Tremont Street side of the Common, already a popular promenade beneath two rows of young trees. Here Bostonians take the air, singly and in groups, while beyond a lively panorama of 18th-century civic life is seen. At the far left is the Powder House, and the three small houses beyond stand on land owned by the painter John Singleton Copley. At the far right is the beacon giving the hill its name. Based on a 1768 watercolor by Christian Remick, this engraving was published in 1902 by Charles E. Goodspeed. It is our earliest view of the Colonial pasture and military training field. (Courtesy BPL.)

For some 150 years, the Hancock House lorded over the Common. Built in 1737 by the merchant Thomas Hancock, it was inherited 27 years later by his nephew John. It played a key role in events surrounding the Revolution. When John Hancock was in hiding under sentence of death, the mansion was occupied by royal troops. The house was torn down in 1863 despite desperate efforts to save it. (Courtesy FPG.)

When John Hancock moved into his uncle's stone mansion, he was already known as one of the leading rebels in Boston. A signer of the Declaration of Independence, he later served nine years as the first governor of Massachusetts. In addition to planting trees on the Beacon Street side of the Common, he erected a bandstand there and hired musicians to give public concerts. (Courtesy BPL.)

19

During the winter of 1775–1776, the Common was an armed camp with an entrenched garrison of almost 2,000 Redcoats. Seen above, this image shows a detail of a view from Beacon Hill, which comes from a series of English military drawings. To the right of two British officers is the Hancock House, and on their left is the Common. Its shoreline was the point from which British troops had embarked for Lexington and Concord. (Courtesy Massachusetts Historical Society.)

Some 20 years later, in a view from the same hillside, the Great Elm stands guard over a tranquil Common, again at peace. Small boats ply the Back Bay waters, and to the south along Tremont Street, the double row of trees forms the beginning of a proper mall. This view first appeared in the November 1790 issue of *Massachusetts Magazine*. (Courtesy Boston Athenaeum.)

On October 30, 1799, Boston celebrated the birthday of John Adams with a review of troops on the Common. Such military displays were a popular form of entertainment, drawing large crowds of citizens from all walks of life. The activities in the foreground reveal the holiday mood. This is our earliest image of the Massachusetts State House, designed by 24-year-old Charles Bulfinch and completed the previous year. (Courtesy BPL.)

By the end of the century, great changes were under way on Beacon Hill. In 1795, the Commonwealth had acquired a portion of John Hancock's former pasture, and three years later, Bulfinch's new Massachusetts State House was complete. Its majestic façade would dominate many future views of the Common, and it would become the model for state capitol buildings across the new nation. (Courtesy Boston Athenaeum.)

The image of the Massachusetts State House and the Common soon became a familiar decorative motif on untold numbers of ceramic pitchers, platters, and plates produced by English manufacturers for export to America. This Staffordshire platter, made by Joseph Stubbs (1790–1829), is a handsome example. (Courtesy Historic New England/SPNEA.)

This fine early view of the Mall dates from about 1800, when Tremont Street still resembled a country lane. The image is from a watercolor attributed to Lucy Knox, daughter of the American general Henry Knox, whose home was nearby. Some of the Mall's trees (left) are now mature, the outer row having been planted in 1725. Just visible along the rustic split-rail fence is an arched entry near today's West Street—the first formal entrance to the grounds. For many years, the most popular part of the Common, the Mall, was destroyed by subway construction in the 1890s. (Courtesy BPL.)

The image above dates from 1804, the one below from four years later. In both views, Beacon Street is becoming lined with large brick residences. Though still bucolic, the Common fields are now encircled by the town. Cows and townspeople share the fields, and though the Great Elm still dominates the landscape, new trees have been planted along the paths. The row of English elm trees along the future Beacon Street Mall (below) are almost certainly those set out by John Hancock after the Revolution. The house at the extreme left of this image was built by John Phillips, the first mayor of Boston, and was the birthplace of his son Wendell of abolitionist fame. (Above, courtesy FPG; below, courtesy BPL.)

In 1813, the cows graze peacefully beneath the Great Elm, drinking the waters of the muddy ponds that drain into the Back Bay. Row houses line lower Beacon Street, and at the far left is a rare view of the ropewalks that once stood along the shoreline—now the site of the Public Garden. This view, by James Kidder, appeared in the June 1813 issue of *Polyanthos* magazine. (Courtesy FPG.)

When the Marquis de Lafayette made his 1824 tour of America, Boston gave him a huge reception with a military review and dinner for 1,200 on the Common. A century later, the Tremont Street Mall was renamed in his honor, and this tablet by John F. Paramino was set up near Park Street station. The photographer apparently took this image when the monument was newly installed. (Courtesy Historic New England/SPNEA.)

A View of the Back Bay - Charles Street & the Common from a sketch taken in 1823 from the Balcony of 61 Beacon St by M.J.D. Boston

This 1823 view of the corner of Charles and Beacon gives a final glimpse of a rural Common. All cows were banned from these acres seven years later, and in the same decade, the wood fence was replaced with one of decorative iron. The boathouse likely served as the headquarters of the Sea Fencibles, a naval militia group known locally as the Sea Dogs. This building also disappeared as the city began filling the Back Bay shoreline. According to the legend at the bottom of the drawing, the sketch was made from the balcony of a house at 61 Beacon Street by Mary Jane Peabody Derby. (Courtesy BPL.)

Three

PLEASURE GROUND

By the mid-19th century, these acres would be transformed from pasture to pleasure ground—to a "park" in the modern sense of the word. At the same time, improvements in the printing process encouraged artists to create works for reproduction, and the Common became a favorite theme for local printmakers. As lithography flourished during the 1830s and 1840s, the visual picture becomes more complete.

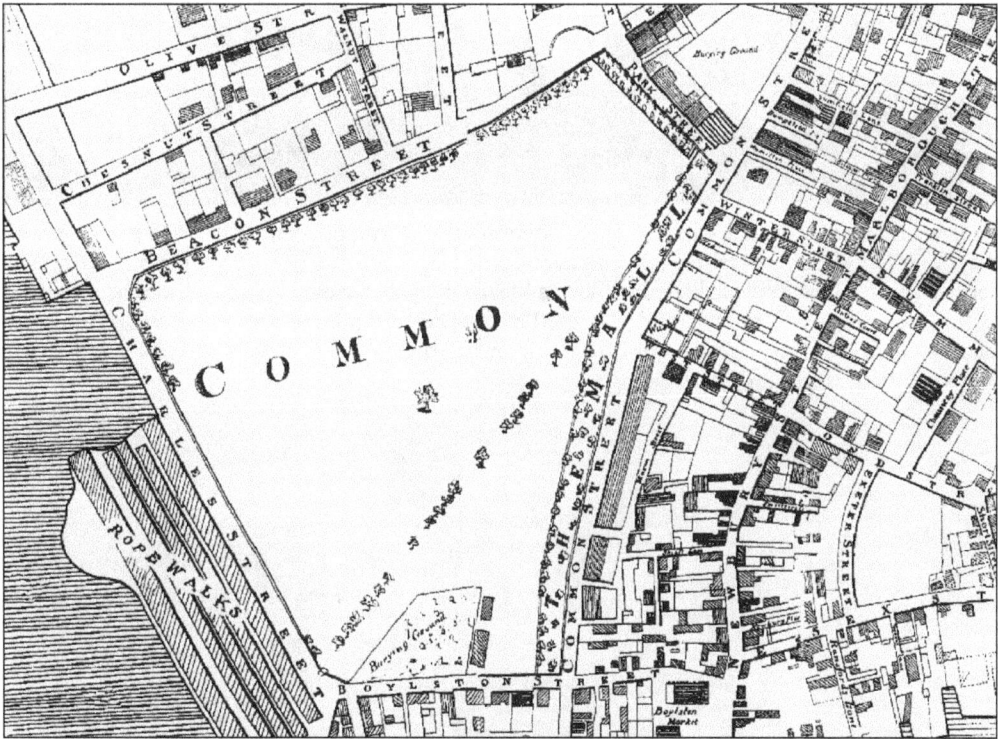

The modern street plan of Beacon Hill is now in place, and the Back Bay shore has been extended to create dry land for ropewalks (see page 25). The Common itself is partially defined by malls, and a planting of shade trees lines a path crossing from Charles to Common (Tremont) Street. The map is a detail, slightly modified, of the 1814 Hales Map of Boston. (Courtesy FPG.)

In this lithograph by James Kidder, the Common's transformation into a wooded park is under way. The Great Elm, at the far left, has been joined by neat rows of younger trees flanking the footpaths that have replaced the meandering trails in earlier views. At the Park-Beacon corner is the 1804 Amory-Ticknor House, designed by Charles Bulfinch and still standing. The scene dates from 1829. James Kidder was one of a growing number of professional artists working in Boston by this time. (Courtesy BPL.)

By the early 1830s, the Tremont Street Mall had become a place of fashion and leisure. With a new awareness of the benefits of fresh air and exercise, Bostonians took to the malls to promenade. Certain gentlemen began each day with a brisk one-mile walk around the Common—a tradition continued by modern-day joggers. This lovely watercolor is by the English-born painter George Harvey. (Courtesy Bostonian Society/Old State House.)

In 1835, George Harvey left for New York, where he became identified with the Hudson River School. There, he painted a series of "atmospheric landscapes," including this view of the Common. On the Parade Ground, scythers hone their blades and men pitch hay onto a cart. A rainbow frames the 1809 Park Street Church. (Courtesy New York Historical Society.)

Balloon ascensions were among the earliest in the extraordinary chronicle of public events on the 19th-century Common. Here, in September 1834, spectators watch from wagons and coaches and others crowd the lawn and rooftop to witness the ascent of a balloonist named Charles F. Durand. The large square building is perhaps the amphitheater erected at the foot of the Common mentioned about this time. (Courtesy Bostonian Society/Old State House.)

From this time forward, images of children (almost always boys) using the Common's fields for sports and games are encountered. In addition to baseball and football, cricket and field hockey were played. This woodcut shows Boston boys of the 1830s playing a game that looks strikingly like modern baseball. In fact, this is said to be one of the earliest known images of the game. (Courtesy Bostonian Society/Old State House.)

30

"View of Part of the Old Mall, with the Contemplated Iron Fence" is reprinted from the July 1835 issue of *The American Magazine of Useful and Entertaining Knowledge*. The Tremont Street Mall, now a century old, is shaded by three rows of large and graceful trees shading two parallel walks. The mile-long fence was finished in December, completely enclosing the Common. The area in the foreground of this view is now occupied by the entrance kiosks to the Park Street subway station. (Courtesy Boston Athenaeum.)

Grand Centennial March.
As performed by the
BOSTON BANDS.
Composed & respectfully dedicated to the
HON. HARRISON GRAY OTIS,
Mayor of Boston
BY
CH: ZEUNER.

BOSTON.
Published by C. Bradlee 164 Washington Street
1830.

Illustrated sheet music covers proliferated after 1830. Since Boston was a center for both music publishing and lithography, local scenes on music sheets were not unusual. "Grand Centennial March," published in 1830, features an image closely related to George Harvey's watercolor of the same period (see page 29). The music sheet was dedicated to Boston's popular mayor (and Beacon Street resident) Harrison Gray Otis. The familiar scene includes no cows; it was Mayor Otis who banned them the year this music sheet was published. (Courtesy Boston Athenaeum.)

In July 1834, the fledgling Whig Party erected an immense pavilion on the Common. The tent, which could hold 2,500 people, was supported by a grand "liberty pole" eighty feet in height. This pole supposedly remained on the Common for many years; perhaps it was put to use as the flagstaff that was erected "near the Great Tree" a few years later. (Courtesy FPG.)

Another picturesque event from the era was the 1844 convention of the New England Order of Washingtonians, an early temperance group of reformed drinkers. They paraded the Common under military escort singing, "The teetotalers are coming with the Cold Water Pledge." Then, before thousands of witnesses, they consecrated themselves to Temperance reform. (Courtesy Bostonian Society/Old State House.)

"The National Lancers with the Reviewing Officers on Boston Common" records one of the military displays that became increasingly popular as years passed. Here, in August 1837, the smartly dressed cavalry company parades near the Frog Pond. Dozens of such volunteer militia companies were in Boston during these years. In addition to providing popular entertainment, they performed a role similar to that of the modern National Guard. The Lancers, for example, would play an important part in maintaining order and protecting property after the Great Fire of 1872. This lithograph is an early work by the marine painter Fitz Hugh Lane. (Courtesy FPG.)

"Boston Common, the most beautiful park in the world," pronounces the caption below this 1842 view by Boston artist Hammett Billings. The venerable elm, now protected by an iron fence, is at the height of its beauty. Behind it is the flagstaff, which stood beside the Frog Pond until it was moved to Powder House Hill. (Courtesy Boston Athenaeum.)

Meanwhile, the modern age was dawning. In 1835, two railroad companies completed tracks across the Back Bay. At the foot of the Common, a train of the Boston and Providence line approaches its station in Park Square, while a Boston and Worcester locomotive steams westward across the flats. (Courtesy FPG.)

The once muddy Frog Pond, curbed and ornamented with a fountain, became the centerpiece of the mid-19th-century Common. The fountain, installed in 1848, was in many ways the symbol of the modern Boston. Its debut was the highlight of the extravagant daylong Water Celebration, seen here, hailing the introduction of the city's public water system. In his 1910 book *Boston Common*, Mark Anthony DeWolfe Howe vividly described the scene: "When the water was turned on, and the fountain leaped high into the air, the school-children, assembled with representatives of every other element of the population, sang Lowell's Ode, written for the occasion, beginning 'My Name Is Water'; the bells rang, cannon were fired, rockets soared aloft." (Courtesy Boston Athenaeum.)

Four

THE GOLDEN AGE

If Boston Common had a golden age, it was the mid-years of the 19th century. "The Athens of America" revered its ancient Common as a precious heritage. The richest sources of images from this period are the wood engravings prepared for the "pictorials," the illustrated weekly magazines that flourished in the 1850s. Boston-based *Gleason's Pictorial Drawing-Room Companion* (renamed *Ballou's Pictorial* in 1855) published dozens of Common scenes.

In a popular lithograph by John Bachman, the Common and a young Public Garden appear in 1850 as the centerpiece of a thriving city. The original peninsula is now fully developed, and with the creation of the Public Garden, the reclamation of the Back Bay has begun. This bird's-eye view is a somewhat fanciful image, but it correctly records the Common's paths, its malls, and the new Frog Pond fountain. (Courtesy FPG.)

While sedate citizens stroll and chat, their children and their dogs run freely. First known as Cochituate Fountain, it was named for the Natick lake that was the source of Boston's new water supply. *Gleason's* reported that its jet, nearly 95 feet high, "forms a pure and sparkling column. . . . It is seldom that its twilight performance is not witnessed by a large and delighted audience." (Courtesy Boston Athenaeum.)

The May 10, 1851, issue of *Gleason's* gives a lively description of a popular annual event: "The First of May, or May Morning, has, for a long period, been a sort of gala occasion for the firemen of Boston, when the companies would turn out to try their skill, and the power of their respective engines with each other, in throwing water over the flag-staff in the Common, and in sprinkling the assembled multitude by way of a dessert to their performance." (Courtesy Boston Athenaeum.)

On a small hill near Boylston Street was "Smokers Circle," a retreat reserved for the gentlemanly users of tobacco. At the time, smoking was forbidden on city streets and elsewhere on the Common. This scene appeared in an 1851 issue of *Gleason's*. (Courtesy Boston Athenaeum.)

In September 1851, a three-day extravaganza known as the Railroad Jubilee celebrated two important local events: the beginning of rail service to Canada and the launching of transatlantic steamship service to Liverpool. The honored guests included Millard Fillmore and Canadian governor-general Lord Elgin. The immense dinner tent, said to accommodate 3,600, was erected near the Tremont Street Mall. (Courtesy Boston Athenaeum.)

At an antislavery rally in 1851, the abolitionist Wendell Phillips addressed a gathering of black and white citizens. An unsympathetic *Gleason's* noted that authorities had moved the crowd ("heated partisans . . . ranting and threatening") from the grounds of the Massachusetts State House to the Common. The scene foreshadowed the events of the next decade, as the slavery issue intensified and the nation moved toward war. (Courtesy FPG.)

In July 1852, huzzas rang for the aging Daniel Webster as thousands of supporters lined a parade route that ended at the Common. The cavalcade was the largest ever seen in Boston, according to *Gleason's*. Here Webster addresses the crowd from a raised platform. Later the ailing statesman assured a well-wisher that "I intend to live as long as I can." He died in October. (Courtesy Boston Athenaeum.)

Military reviews and parades continued to be popular pictorial subjects. They were also enormously popular with the public, and, in time, admission to some events was limited to ticket holders. The image above records the visit of the First Battalion of Rifles of West Newbury, which was enthusiastically reported by the local press. The scene, from 1853, shows the iron fence along the Charles Street Mall; beyond the lands of the Public Garden have been partially filled. Below is a scene from the previous year, when about 250 men of the 5th Regiment of Artillery encamped for two days near the corner of Charles and Beacon Streets. *Gleason's* reported that when illuminated at night, the camp presented "a very beautiful and novel sight." (Above, courtesy Dr. Michael C. Stone; below, courtesy Boston Athenaeum.)

One of the most extravagant militia events of the period was in honor of the Hungarian patriot Louis Kossuth, who made a triumphal tour of the country in 1852. In May, he arrived in Boston, where he spoke at Faneuil Hall and then reviewed some 2,000 troops on the Common. According to *Gleason's*, he was received with great popular enthusiasm, with 60,000 onlookers crowding the nearby malls and the slopes of Flagstaff Hill. (Courtesy Dr. Michael C. Stone.)

Promenade concerts, the rage in Europe and England, had arrived in Boston by 1856. In August, *Ballou's Pictorial* enthusiastically reported: "During the present season, our beautiful Common has been rendered doubly attractive on fine evenings, by the performance of excellent music by our principal bands, which are not matched by those of any city in the Union. In the center, among the trees, are the staging and band. Grouped around the base, standing or promenading, are representatives of all classes of our population." (Courtesy Boston Athenaeum.)

In 1855, a new steam-powered fire engine, the "Miles Greenwood," arrived in Boston from Cincinnati, and the March 31 issue of *Ballou's* described its debut: "For the trial a large space was roped off at the corner of Tremont and Park Streets, and only those furnished with invitations were admitted to the enclosure." Competing against hand-pumped engines, the "Miles Greenwood" was deemed "decidedly superior," winning every trial. (Courtesy Boston Athenaeum.)

By the 1850s, the Common, now surrounded by residential neighborhoods, had become a natural playground for children. Reminiscences of local boys abound with references to the Common: swimming and fishing in the Back Bay, skating on the Frog Pond, kiting, and playing team sports. According to tradition, during the British occupation, a group of boys complained to General Gage that the presence of troops on the Common was interfering with their coasting. Gage decreed that the boys could resume sledding, sometimes joined, it is said, by British soldiers. In this scene from 1857, youngsters celebrate the season near the Great Elm. In his 1962 memoir *One Boy's Boston*, Samuel Eliot Morison recounts that girls also coasted: "[M]y mother told me how she had a sled named 'General McClellan' [all sleds were named in those days] which was much admired, but the time came when other children pointed at it and hooted, so she ran home crying and had a piece of carpet tacked over the then disreputable name." (Courtesy Boston Athenaeum.)

44

When snow covered the Common, the steep slopes favored sledding. In this 1856 illustration from *Ballou's Pictorial*, pedestrians make way for sleds racing down "the Long Coast" from the corner of Park and Beacon Streets to the Tremont Street Mall. The sleds are identified by name; here "Minnehaha" bears down on "Old Ironsides." (Courtesy Fred Mauet.)

Two decades later, coasting had become more elaborate, with toboggan-like "double rippers" carrying up to 10 adult passengers. The coasts were sprinkled at night to make the ice smooth for the next day. For a time, the paths were roped off for safety with wooden footbridges for pedestrians. However, there were still frequent accidents, and this kind of coasting was eventually halted. (Courtesy FPG.)

The three Winslow Homer works on these pages appeared in illustrated weeklies in the late 1850s. Homer spent several years working for a Boston lithographic firm and knew the Common firsthand. Above is a lively scene from *Ballou's Pictorial* in 1857. Set alongside the Frog Pond on a windswept day, it is very similar to the view on page 38. A comparison of the two images, however, shows not only Homer's talents but also what has happened to the style of magazine illustration during the decade. Below is Homer's view of the Beacon Street Mall, which has begun to vie with the Tremont Street Mall as a place of fashion. It appeared in *Harper's Weekly* in 1858. (Both courtesy FPG.)

Patriotic occasions raised civic enthusiasm to a pitch, and the Fourth of July was traditionally a time of rowdy entertainments. The malls, crowded with attractions, resembled a county fair midway. Tents and booths dispensed candy, cakes, and copious amounts of alcoholic beverages. The day concluded with a flare of fireworks. In this view by Homer, the vendor in the foreground seems to be "Apple Mary," who appears in several photographs during the next decade. Nathaniel Hawthorne's *American Notebooks* include a colorful description of the Fourth on the Common: "On the top of one of the booths a monkey, with a tail two or three feet long. . . . There are boys going about with molasses candy, almost melted down in the sun. Shows: A mammoth rat; a collection of pirates, murderers and the like, in wax. . . . One or two old salts, rather the worse for liquor; in general the people are temperate." (Courtesy Boston Athenaeum.)

These happy scenes were interrupted by the outbreak of the Civil War. The Common, once the site of abolitionist rallies, now witnessed the grim phases of war. This 1862 illustration shows the headquarters of the local recruiting committee at Flagstaff Hill, where 15 years later, the memorial to the war's dead would be erected. (Courtesy FPG.)

Five

THE COMMON IN FOCUS

Images from the pictorial magazines portrayed an idyllic Common animated by attractive, happy citizens. But in the early photographs from the same period, these scenes lose some of their glamour, as awkward little figures move against bleak landscapes. Happily photography arrived in time to record the final days of two legendary subjects: the Great Elm and the Hancock House. And soon comes the fascination of real-life images of ordinary citizens passing before the camera's eye.

Dating from the mid-1850s, this panoramic view southwest from the dome of the Massachusetts State House is likely the earliest photographic image of Boston Common. Across Flagstaff Hill, the once-treeless fields are now thick with greenery, obscuring the view of the Frog Pond and malls. On the right is a corner of the Parade Ground. (Courtesy Boston Athenaeum.)

Probably the earliest photograph taken on the Common, this daguerreotype is known as "An Unidentified Muster." The work of the Boston firm Southworth and Hawes, it is dated to the early 1850s, when the firm was still making daguerreotypes. Daguerreotype group portraits of more than 10 people are extremely rare. While most of the men stood still enough to present a clear image, the American flag behind them is a mere blur. When the partnership dissolved in 1861, Josiah Johnson Hawes struck out on his own, and his architectural photographs of the city streets form an invaluable archive of 19th-century Boston. (Courtesy Historic New England/SPNEA.)

A decade later, sailors from the Russian ships *Vitiar* and *Osliaba* pose along the opposite slope of Flagstaff Hill. By rough count, some 200 Russians are pictured, along with various dignitaries and many spectators in the rear. The squadron visited the Atlantic ports in 1863. The sailors were welcomed ashore by boys of the Latin and English schools with "a reception and a collation." (Courtesy U.S. Naval Historical Center.)

In October 1860, Bostonians turned out in force to welcome the Prince of Wales, the future Edward VII. Here the crowd awaits his arrival near Boylston Street. He later reviewed troops on the Common riding Black Prince, the horse that would serve as model for Washington's mount in the equestrian statue in the Public Garden. (Courtesy Historic New England/SPNEA.)

Midway through the Civil War years, the former daguerreotypist Josiah Johnson Hawes made a glass-plate photograph of military recruits drilling on the Common. Yet to receive their uniforms, they resemble a troupe of ragged schoolboys, especially when compared with the smart militia companies portrayed by the pictorials of the previous decade. Hawes often adopted this round format, using the image as it was projected by the circular lens of the camera, though he did employ square compositions as well. (Courtesy Boston Athenaeum.)

52

In 1863, a coastal storm uncovered the remains of a Colonial-period transatlantic vessel thought to be the *Sparrowhawk*, a ship en route from England to Virginia when it was wrecked off Cape Cod in 1626. The hull was salvaged and reassembled, then exhibited in several American cities. In 1865, while on the Common, it was photographed by Josiah Johnson Hawes. The ship can still be seen at Pilgrim Hall in Plymouth. (Note in the foreground the shadows of the photographer and bystanders, as well as the camera.) (Courtesy BPL.)

The Hancock House remained standing long enough to be properly photographed. This striking image dates from 1863, the year it was torn down. The public outrage that followed sounded the beginnings of Boston's preservationist movement. The women posing on the balcony may be members of the Hancock family, which still owned the house at this time. (Courtesy Bostonian Society/Old State House.)

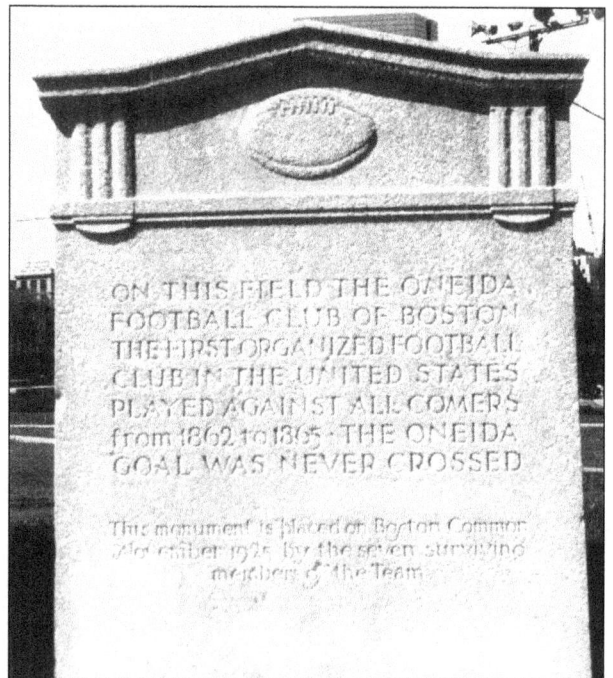

The tablet at the edge of the Parade Ground commemorates a series of football games played in the 1860s between the Oneida Football Club and "all comers." It was placed here in 1925 by the seven surviving members of the team. The exploits of the Oneida Club are recounted in J. DeW. Lovett's *Old Boston Boys and the Games They Played* (1906). (Photograph by Robert B. Severy Jr.; courtesy Historic New England/SPNEA.)

54

The first piece of public art arrived on the Common in 1868. It bears the name of its donor, Gardner Brewer, who purchased the piece abroad and had it installed within sight of his house—one of the large residences erected along the Beacon Street frontage of the former Hancock property. The fountain is a bronze copy of a French original that won a gold medal at the 1855 Paris World's Fair. Its sculptures represent mythological figures associated with water: Neptune, Amphitrite, Asis, and Galatea. It was later moved to its present location near the Tremont Street Mall. (Courtesy Bostonian Society/Old State House.)

This woman is the best known among the many vendors who conducted business on the Common in the 19th century. Known as "Apple Mary," she was photographed in various parts of the Common in all seasons of the year. Here she sits bundled up along the Beacon Street Mall. The large English elm tree behind her, with its botanical label, must be one of the famous Hancock Elms. (Courtesy BPL.)

Another vendor displays her wares just inside the Boylston-Charles Street gate. Beyond her are the young Public Garden, the redbrick bowfronts that once lined Boylston Street, and the spire of the 1861 Arlington Street Church. Most of these early stereo views look posed—as indeed they were, limited always by the speed of the emulsion available at the time. (Photograph by John Heywood; courtesy Historic New England/SPNEA.)

The stereoscopic views on these pages are all taken from double-image cards like the one pictured above. Seen through a handheld viewer, they produced a three-dimensional effect, and they were immensely popular for several decades. (The arched upper edge usually indicates an earlier date.) In this view, a sign tacked to the tree identifies the lemonade and candy vendor as a disabled veteran. (Courtesy FPG.)

Stereo views provide some unusual images of the 19th-century Common. On the left is our only known photograph of the deer park that stood near the Boylston-Tremont corner from 1863 to 1882. The enclosure also housed peacocks. On the right is another rare view, a scene from the centennial celebration of the Battle of Bunker Hill on June 17, 1875. (Both courtesy Historic New England/SPNEA.)

Of the scores of stereoscopic views of the Common, some are very curious and compelling—intriguing little genre scenes for which there are neither understanding nor explanation. These local characters along the Tremont Street Mall are obviously posing, but who are they? Taken 20 years earlier than pictures of the well-known "Telescope Man" (see page 66), this scene shows another man and another telescope. (Courtesy American Antiquarian Society.)

The Soldiers and Sailors Monument looks down upon a charming vignette taken from a stereo view dated 1880. Well-dressed men and boys stand beside a wheeled cart identified as a "goat tram," with six large rams in harness. Around this same time in Central Park, goat cart rides cost 10¢; the Common's tram must have been a private concession as well. (Stereo view by R. E. Lord; courtesy Historic New England/SPNEA.)

Two young women take refreshment at a cast-iron drinking fountain. Tin dippers suspended by chains were filled with water spouting from the mouths of griffins. Several similar fountains were located on the Common at the time, but all were eventually replaced with the more sanitary bubblers. At the left is a "ghost," the blurred image of a boy in motion. (Courtesy BPL.)

Dating from the era of stovepipe hats, this view shows the Brewer Fountain in its original location; a faint image of the dome of the Massachusetts State House looms above the treetops. The fountain is not flowing, a common condition leading William Dean Howells to lament "its four seasons of severe drought." In a breach of 19th-century decorum, people sit on the grass. (Courtesy American Antiquarian Society.)

These images represent the life and death of a tree. The new cameras did not overlook the Great Elm, which still lived, held in ever-more esteem with the passing years. It was seldom photographed without a cluster of admirers surrounding its protective iron fence. (Courtesy FPG.)

The morning after a severe storm in June 1860, the rumor spread that the Great Elm had fallen. Rushing to the scene, townspeople learned that only one large limb was down. (A cross section of this branch revealed 190 rings.) From this time onward, photographs show the tree to be sadly disfigured, supported by splints and braces. (Courtesy Bostonian Society/Old State House.)

The Great Elm site nevertheless remained a popular place for group portraits. Here several hundred frock-coated Methodist ministers gather beneath its limbs for a photograph in 1872. The tree has just four more years to live. (Courtesy BPL.)

On the stormy night of February 15, 1876, the old tree finally blew down. "The newspapers of the succeeding days are fairly humid with the tears of local poets," reported Mark Anthony DeWolfe Howe. Here the tree is sawed into lengths—some of which were salvaged as souvenirs: small veneered plaques and canes, and even pieces of furniture. (Stereo view by Edwin N. Peabody; courtesy Historic New England/SPNEA.)

Plans for a Civil War memorial were published as early as 1866, and foundations were dug on Flagstaff Hill, but the project was halted for lack of funds. A decade later, work started on another monument (shown below). Sometime between these two dates, the hilltop was occupied by a strange little lean-to called Station Four and a Half. The guards are identified as "Sgt. Winship and Patrolmen Daley and Lucas." (Courtesy American Antiquarian Society.)

The Soldiers and Sailors Monument is now finished, but construction material still litters the site. The architect/sculptor was a talented young Irish-born artist named Martin Milmore, and the cost was $75,000. When the monument was dedicated, on September 17, 1877, Generals McClellan and Hooker were among those attending the ceremonies (along with, in a time of reconciliation, two Confederate officers). (Courtesy American Antiquarian Society.)

In 1888, the Boston Massacre Memorial was dedicated near the Tremont Street Mall. The work of Robert Kraus, its standing bronze figure represents revolution breaking the chains of tyranny. The bas-relief depicting the events before the Old State House on March 5, 1770, features Crispus Attucks, the first to fall. This photograph was taken before 1912, when the old wooden bandstand behind the memorial was replaced. (Courtesy FPG.)

Sometime in the 1870s, this picturesque stick-style cottage was erected near the West Street Gate. The photograph, published in 1910, shows its original size and site. For many years, it served as a ladies' comfort station. In 1992, it was moved, enlarged, and adapted as Boston's Visitors Center and the Common headquarters of the Boston Park Rangers. (Courtesy FPG.)

In 1858, Boston Common made a major literary appearance in Oliver Wendell Holmes's *Autocrat at the Breakfast Table* as the place where the Autocrat courted the Schoolmistress and popped the question: "Will you take the long path with me?" (The Schoolmistress accepted.) The Long Path soon became famous, appearing frequently in stereo views and postcards. Here, several decades later, a group of young women in white summer dresses moves briskly up the Long Path toward the camera. (Courtesy BPL.)

Josiah Johnson Hawes was still photographing the streets of Boston in 1875, when he captured this stunning view on Park Street, looking down the Beacon Street Mall. The New England winter, a favorite theme with the earlier printmakers, became a popular motif for the camera. (Courtesy FPG.)

Most of the people in these early photographs have been anonymous individuals, immortalized by chance through their fleeting appearance within the camera's view. An exception is the Telescope Man, a well-known character of the period. Oliver Wendell Holmes called him "the Galileo of the Mall," and his customers paid 5¢ to climb the small ladder and peer through his lens. The sign tacked to the tripod in the above photograph reads "Sun Spots." Below is another sighting of the Telescope Man. He stands near a Victorian drinking fountain, one of several given to eastern cities in the name of temperance by Dr. Henry Daniel Cogswell of San Francisco. Installed in 1884, it was almost immediately denounced as a reproach to the good taste of the citizens. These voices were soon heeded, and in 1894, the fountain was removed. (Both courtesy Historic New England/SPNEA.)

A man and a boy lean against a fence on a chilly Boston day, the man stoic and seemingly unaware of the camera. The scene is unremarkable, but the crisp stereo image shows in detail several physical features of the 19th-century Common: sturdy rail fences and well-kept gravel paths flanked by cobblestone gutters. The photograph dates from around 1870. (Courtesy BPL.)

By the 1870s, the Charles Street Mall was a half-century old and displaying a rich maturity. Beneath this allée of leafy elms, two boys mounted on tall tricycles pose for the photographer. Glimpsed through the trees on the right is the tower of the 1872 Boston and Providence Railroad station at Park Square. Like the Tremont Street Mall, this shady avenue would eventually be sacrificed to urban "progress." (Courtesy BPL.)

Balloon ascensions grew ever more popular and, by the 1880s, were drawing the largest crowds of the year. In 1892, some 100,000 people witnessed a launch that ended in tragedy when the balloon fell into Boston Harbor, killing two passengers. This undated photograph gives a good idea of the size of the crowds. The group in the foreground looks like the VIP section. (Courtesy Historic New England/SPNEA.)

This peaceful view down Park Street is a reminder that the Common was once surrounded by residential streets. In the foreground is Charles Bulfinch's 1804 Amory-Ticknor House, which still stands today, though much altered. Farther downhill is an ensemble of eight row houses, also by Bulfinch, and Peter Banner's Park Street Church. This photograph has been dated to around 1860. (Courtesy FPG.)

A trio of young women moves gracefully across a frozen Frog Pond, followed by two boys, one of them carrying a large box. This carefully composed image was apparently the work of a serious photographer, for it comes from a collection of lantern slides once owned by the Boston Camera Club. (Courtesy Bostonian Society/Old State House.)

The most acclaimed piece of sculpture on the Common is Augustus Saint-Gaudens's Robert Gould Shaw Memorial. The enormous bas-relief depicts the mounted Shaw leading the Massachusetts 54th Regiment, the first all-volunteer black regiment in the Union army. Colonel Shaw, together with many of his men, died at Fort Wagner, South Carolina, in July 1863. In 1982, the Friends of the Public Garden raised funds to restore and endow the monument, which was rededicated in 1997. Present at the unveiling ceremonies, Saint-Gaudens offered this poignant account: "Many of them were bent and crippled, many with white heads, some with bouquets. . . . The impression of those old soldiers, passing the very spot where they left for war so many years before, thrills me even as I write these words. They faced and saluted the relief, with the music playing 'John Brown's Body.' . . . They seemed as if returning from the war; the troops of bronze marching in the opposite direction in which they had left for the front, and the young men there represented now showing these veterans the vigor and hope of youth. It was a consecration." (Photograph by Thomson and Thomson; courtesy Historic New England/SPNEA.)

Saint-Gaudens was the foremost American sculptor of his day, and after accepting the Shaw Memorial commission in 1884, he took almost 14 years to complete the job. The monument was finally unveiled on May 30, 1897, with ceremonies lasting most of the day. Above a section of the military parade approaches the monument along an unpaved Beacon Street in a light rain. Below the sun is now shining as admirers gather to view the new landmark. The two large elms flanking the monument are at this writing still alive. Their age is uncertain, but this photograph shows that at the end of the 19th century, they were already big trees. (Both courtesy FPG.)

The winter of 1898–1899 was a hard one. Here, near the Shaw Memorial, both man and beast brave the storm to keep Beacon Street open for sleighs. Horses continued to plow paths inside the Common for many more years. (Courtesy Bostonian Society/Old State House.)

According to its caption, this dramatic evening photograph was taken at 8:10 p.m. on November 30, 1898—three days after the Portland Gale, a legendary blizzard of the era. The view shows the wooden bandstand that was replaced in 1912 by the classic Parkman Bandstand. It stood on the site of Cow (or Horse) Pond, which was filled in 1838. (Photograph by H. W. Weller; courtesy Historic New England/SPNEA.)

The intrepid gentleman with the top hat and cane is John C. Ropes, a well-known Boston lawyer who also wrote books on military history. In this crisp, wintry image, he is likely traveling from his office on State Street to his Mount Vernon Street home. (Courtesy Bostonian Society/Old State House.)

Cartloads of snow are hauled through the West Street Gate to be dumped on the Common—a practical solution to the problem of snow piling up on congested downtown streets. The practice continued for years; in fact, one of the arguments given for installing the gate in 1859 was precisely for this purpose. (Courtesy American Antiquarian Society.)

This image of the Tremont Street Mall in its final days shows a busy scene near the West Street Gate. Within a decade, the Mall would be destroyed to make way for subway construction. At that time, it was announced that the gates, with their massive lanterns, would be moved to

the grounds of the former Confederate prison in Andersonville, Georgia—though if they ever arrived there, they have since disappeared. The Telescope Man's telescope stands on the far left. (Courtesy Historic New England/SPNEA.)

Before subway construction began, the Boston Transit Authority created a complete photographic record of all areas of impact. Each section of the iron fences along Boylston and Tremont Streets was numbered and photographed. Many of these images are enlivened by the presence of local characters, apparently attracted by the camera and eager to pose. Along Tremont Street (above), a small group has showed up behind section No. 39. Individual trees were also numbered and photographed, each with a human figure standing nearby to provide scale. Seen on the left is tree No. 501, west of the burying ground. (Both courtesy Historic New England/SPNEA.)

The subway project was a huge undertaking, almost three years from beginning to end—and all the more remarkable because most of the work was done by hand. Here, in March 1895, men assemble near Charles and Boylston Streets seeking employment. A variety of vehicular traffic jams Charles Street. (Courtesy Bostonian Society/Old State House.)

A deep, open trench paralleling Tremont Street is filled with horse-drawn wagons and construction material. On the left, a fine old tree perches at the rim of this man-made precipice, which can be scaled with the ladders propped nearby. The wooden pedestrian bridge that spans the gap near West Street bears a painted sign advertising Waverley Bicycles. (Courtesy Bostonian Society/Old State House.)

A street trolley moves gingerly through this *c.* 1897 work site, a jumble of construction materials and debris. The project rendered large parts of the Common impassable, but beyond the board fence, the Brewer Fountain and the old footpaths appear orderly and serene. There are scores of photographs of this project, not all of them dated. They are arranged on these pages as logically as possible. (Courtesy Library of Congress.)

For pedestrians, traveling in the Common could be a messy business. In January 1896, the former mall is a field of mud between scattered piles of melting snow. (Courtesy Bostonian Society/Old State House.)

Tall trestles supported the elevated rail tracks that traversed the Common from the excavation areas to the Parade Ground, where debris was spread across the open fields near Charles Street. Here a small steam engine pulling four carts returns to the construction site. (Courtesy Bostonian Society/Old State House.)

In 1897, sidewalk superintendents gather as a mason works to buttress the great granite slabs that form the outer walls of the Boylston Street subway entrance. Beneath the exposed beams is the new subway tunnel, which formed the first link in Boston's modern transit system—and the first subway in the country. (Courtesy Bostonian Society/Old State House.)

On a summer day in 1906, the new mall has a fresh but finished look. The entrance kiosks were denounced by a local critic as "a series of stone coverings for unrelated holes in the surface of the Mall." At the end, it seems that the Boston Transit Authority had chosen to economize on the design of the kiosk ensemble, which originally called for colonnades with "seats, posts, and other architectural features"—including the Brewer Fountain, which was to be moved to the spot. It was the end of an era. A passage in the 1930 *Fifty Years of Boston* laments the changes to the Common in the past half century: "Goat carts for children were barred from the Charles Street Mall [before 1890]. The delightful old broken-down apple women who sat under the elm trees were ordered off the Common forever with their baskets of fruit and candy about the time the martins and swallows departed the city. Shortly thereafter the deer park was abolished; and an astronomer with his long brass telescope, pointed at the daylight sky, disappeared." (Courtesy Library of Congress.)

Six

WARS AND PEACE

Tracking images of the Common into the 20th century, one finds a rich new source in the daily press. Of the 11 dailies published in Boston in 1910, many had a staff photographer and presses that could print front-page images. By this time, cameras were also available to a growing number of amateur photographers. Armed with these lightweight portable devices, people were taking unposed snapshots—a fresh, new way of seeing the Common.

A slice of Boston's modern new skyline, backed by the 1915 Custom House Tower, rises behind this c. 1920 view of the old burying ground. By this time, Tremont Street has assumed its commercial character. The little tin lizzies moving up Boylston Street look harmless enough, but they portend the day when the automobile will have enormous impact on the periphery of the Common. (Courtesy BPL.)

The first decade of the 20th century saw the astonishment of flight, and in December 1909, Lincoln Beachey demonstrated his "airship," a gas-filled bag with a framework carrying a motor, controls, and the suspended pilot. Ballooning led to aeroplanes, which Beachey flew in daredevil style, zooming under Niagara Falls and astonishing America with spiral and death glides before his fatal crash into San Francisco Bay in 1915 at age 31. (Courtesy BPL.)

On January 2, 1913, Harry M. Jones became the first to land a plane on the Common. Thinking he had won a $20,000 prize offered by Boston newspapers, he was told, "Sorry, that was last year." He then flew on, carrying in his 1911 Wright Model B Flyer the first air parcel post, a shipment of Boston baked beans, to New York City. (Courtesy BPL.)

Ever since the Common ceased being a pasture, the grass has needed mowing, and the earliest image of haying dates to shortly after 1830 (see page 29). Well into the 20th century, hay was still being cut so that new grass could be seeded for the Common's continuing hard use as a city park. The cured hay—as much as 40 tons of it—was then sent to the city stables. (Both courtesy Bostonian Society/Old State House.)

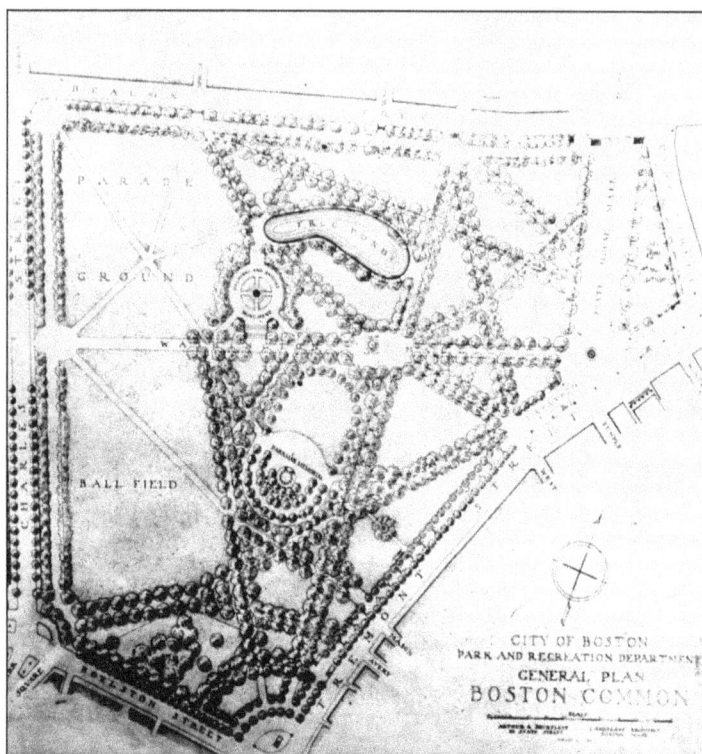

In 1911, the well-known landscape architect Arthur Shurcliff drew up a more formal plan for the Common, with trees defining and screening specific areas. The Parade Ground remains; the Ball Field is a new designation. Trees encircle the Soldiers and Sailors Monument, the Parkman Bandstand, and the site of the Great Elm. Most of Shurcliff's design was executed and much survives. (Courtesy Boston Parks and Recreation Department.)

To carry out the Shurcliff plan, many mature trees were simply moved within the Common. Techniques for shifting trees were developed in the 18th century and practiced later by landscape designers like Frederick Law Olmsted. The tree's root-ball was staved up like a barrel—and sweat and horses did the rest. (Courtesy Frederick Law Olmsted National Historic Site.)

A common like Boston's was, by definition, planted by nature's careless rapture with native trees. In New England, the hardwoods ran to elm, oak, maple, beech, and ash. To enjoy and study specimen trees from foreign climes, Bostonians could stroll in the Public Garden or drive out to the Arnold Arboretum. But the Common could boast at least one exotic—the tall gingko—a native of eastern China, seen here around 1915 in the left foreground, framing the view down the Beacon Street Mall. This tree had been moved to the Common in 1835 from the Pemberton Hill garden of Gardiner Greene and lived until 1975. (Courtesy FPG.)

The Common's first and greatest benefactor was George Francis Parkman. When he died in 1908, he left $5 million for the care of the Common and other city parks. His Greek Revival row house at 33 Beacon Street, once the Parks Department headquarters, is now used by the mayor of Boston for official receptions. (Courtesy Boston Athenaeum.)

The Parkman Bandstand, in the form of a classical temple, was dedicated in 1912. Bandstand concerts still take place here, with listeners sitting on benches circling the stage. But the bandstand also gave the Common its most useful forum for public speaking. Restored in 1996, it has served as the stage for the annual Shakespeare on the Common productions, along with other events. (Courtesy Boston Parks and Recreation Department.)

James Michael Curley, looking imperial and filling the void of the Parkman Bandstand with the honeyed voice he learned at the Staley College of the Spoken Word, had recently been elected mayor of Boston in 1914, when this photograph was taken. Grit in the teeth of the Yankee establishment, he was reelected three times. Novelist Edwin O'Connor memorialized him and his brand of politics in *The Last Hurrah*, published in 1956. This is the first of many Leslie Jones photographs reprinted on these pages. Jones worked for the *Boston Herald Traveler* for 39 years and, in the 1970s, presented his rich archive to the Boston Public Library. (Courtesy BPL, Leslie Jones Collection.)

The flat part of the Common at the bottom of Beacon Hill proved ample space for schoolboy games. Private day schools within walking distance of the Common used it as their athletic field for football and baseball. Notice the teachers, or fathers, gathered around the edge of play on this October 1909 day. One Beacon Street residence has lowered its awnings against the afternoon sun. (Courtesy Library of Congress.)

Through the centuries, the Common has known the displacement brought by war. The generation that fought in the Civil War returned periodically to muster in remembrance of the fallen; likewise, on May 13, 1916, veterans of the Grand Army of the Republic decorated the Soldiers and Sailors Monument. (Courtesy BPL, Leslie Jones Collection.)

Near the burying ground, Civil War veteran P. R. Barker of Fitzgerald, Georgia, tells stories to Boston schoolchildren in August 1924. Kneeling behind him is John Houlder, also a veteran from Fitzgerald. (Courtesy BPL, Leslie Jones Collection.)

Tableaux vivants, French for "living pictures," were enormously popular as home entertainments or civic endeavors, and none more satisfying to all ages than a depiction of the American flag. The 45 stars date this one to pre-1908. Some flags were done entirely by children dressed in colored paper—red and white for the stripes and blue for the ground. The Common flag in this photograph shows women in white hats and dresses, and perhaps in red as well, for the woman in the center foreground wears a dark dress and holds onto a flat hat. Access to one's position was by stairs seen to the right. In the foreground, a policeman patrols. In front of him, a woman clutches a "Box Brownie." (Photograph by Leon Dadmun; courtesy Historic New England/SPNEA.)

On almost any pleasant summer day, the benches on the Common were occupied by well-dressed men reading their newspapers. In this *c.* 1910 photograph, a pair of bootblacks are at work. If enlarged, the image is sharp enough to read the headline on the nearest newspaper, which refers to a local murder case. (Courtesy Historic New England/SPNEA.)

The date is now August 3, 1914, and these straw-hatted men are possibly reading about the outbreak in Europe of what was to be known as the Great War or, when America joined the fighting in 1917, as "the War to End All Wars." Note the mixture of transportation along Tremont Street, as the horse-drawn gives way to the horseless. (Courtesy Historic New England/SPNEA.)

The newest war has hit home. A blimp marked BE (British Expeditionary) Army is tethered on the Common to gather support for the Victory Loan Drive. Balloons were first used in the Franco-Prussian War of 1871 to gather military intelligence through binoculars. Although the Common never saw a battle, it trained soldiers for the Civil War (see page 52) and would now fight on the home front, raising money through liberty bond drives and plowing up land for victory gardens. (Courtesy Massachusetts Historical Society.)

The top French general, Joseph Jacques Césaire Joffre, visited Boston in 1917 to urge American support. Commander-in-chief of the French forces, he had won the Battle of the Marne in 1914 and survived Verdun in 1916; he would serve as the chairman of the Allied War Council from 1916 to 1918. The plight of French war orphans appealed to children everywhere, and little New Englanders contributed from their pocket money. Here, on the Common dais, Joffre listens to Mary Curley's message as her father, Mayor James Michael Curley, watches the text. (Courtesy BPL, Leslie Jones Collection.)

The Common soon became a village of small portable buildings devoted to various aspects of the war effort. Most were provided by the E. F. Hodgson Company of Boston and New York. From left to right, as pictured in the firm's catalogue, are the Food Facts Bureau, Boston Women's Committee on Food Conservation, Massachusetts Public Safety Committee and

The victory gardens were laid out south of the "liberty cottages" shown above. They were practical, feeding those in need, but also educational, as they schooled the home gardener. Nearby was a henhouse and yard. The photograph of the straw-hatted men inspecting the beans and cabbages became a postcard published in 1918 by E. H. Washburn. (Courtesy Bostonian Society/Old State House.)

94

Women's Municipal League, Civic Federation, and the American Red Cross. The Great War would launch volunteerism as a career for women who did not work outside the home, and this setting, with trellised gardens, patriotic flags, and awnings on the "cottages," was attractive and safe. (Courtesy Historic New England/SPNEA.)

Elsewhere on the Common were other cottages and huts devoted to the war effort. Opposite West Street was Liberty Hall, shown camouflaged, where liberty bonds were sold. From its front steps, professional and amateur actors, actresses, and singers called out to passers-by, urging them to support the war effort by buying bonds. (Courtesy Bostonian Society/Old State House.)

When the war was won and the troops came home in 1919, grand parades ran along Tremont Street, and the rain did not matter. Above the canopied reviewing stand on the right, office workers lean precariously forward to take in the scene. (Courtesy BPL, Leslie Jones Collection.)

In the years after the war, school cadets muster on the Parade Ground. For many years, the cadets, a regiment of boys from various Boston high schools, gave annual performances on the Common. As seen in this photograph, it was a popular event, with parents, siblings, and friends coming out to see the schoolboys in their smart military dress. (Courtesy BPL.)

As late as 1927, a captured German gun stood near the Soldiers and Sailors Monument on Flagstaff Hill—a perfect perch for this group of boys, who look as if they have come up from the Frog Pond to pose. (Courtesy BPL, Leslie Jones Collection.)

Delivering a typewriter across the Common in January 1917, sixteen-year-old Louis A. Caulfield earned $6 for a six-day week. This photograph came from the records of the National Child Labor Committee, which noted that Caulfield, of Dorchester, carried the heavy machine about a half-mile. (Courtesy Library of Congress.)

Several years later, with the redbrick Park Street Church their background, young bootblacks wait for customers. The Blackstone Memorial Tablet behind them had been dedicated in 1913. This photograph, taken by Samuel Chamberlain, is one of a series of postcards called The American Series, published in the 1920s. (Courtesy Peabody-Essex Museum.)

Fenway Park it was not, but neither were they the Red Sox (or the Boston Braves) as players took to the two diamonds along Charles Street one cold spring day about 1918. The lengthening shadows on the outfield tell that it is late afternoon, and the spectators lining the fence along the pathway seem to be businessmen on their way home from work. Amateur-league baseball still thrives on the Common, with businesses and hospitals fielding teams, along with a popular Little League program for children from Beacon Hill, Back Bay, and other surrounding neighborhoods. (Courtesy BPL, Leslie Jones Collection.)

Peace in Europe did not insure peace at home. In 1919, about 80 percent of the Boston police force went on strike for better wages. Calvin Coolidge, governor of Massachusetts, called in the militia, and police and their sympathizers were arrested at the Brewer Fountain on the Tremont Street side of the Common. Quashing a rebellion of public servants brought Coolidge to national attention. Elected Warren G. Harding's vice president, he became president when Harding died in office in August 1923, serving until 1929. (Courtesy BPL, Leslie Jones Collection.)

The crash of 1929 and the Great Depression that followed were almost a decade off when the Parkman Bandstand became an auction block. The year is 1921, and the "victims" are unemployed Bostonians who have not been able to find any kind of work on their own. (Courtesy BPL, Leslie Jones Collection.)

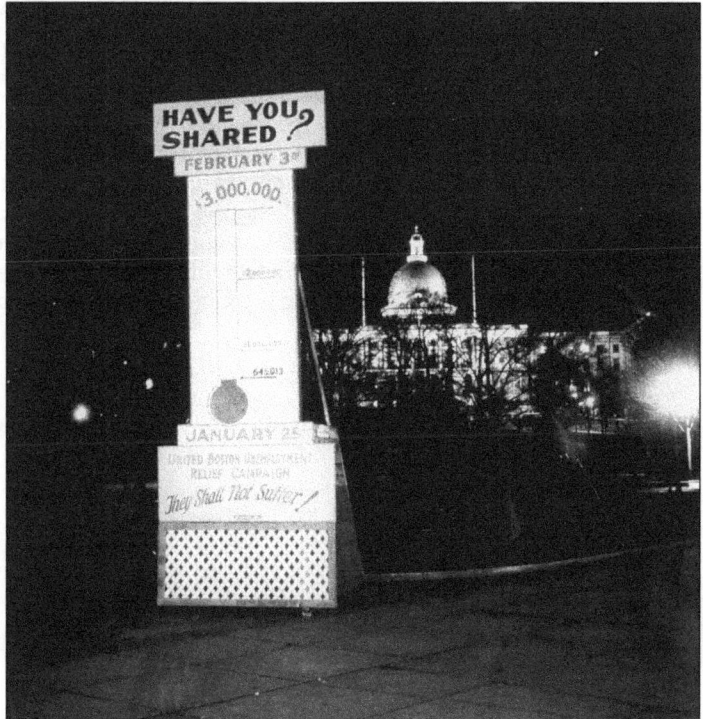

"They Shall Not Suffer" is the motto of the Great Depression fund-raising thermometer erected near Tremont Street in January 1932 by the United Boston Unemployment Relief Campaign. At this point, the campaign seems to have raised about a quarter of its $3 million goal. In the background, the Massachusetts State House façade is now being illuminated at night. (Courtesy BPL, Leslie Jones Collection.)

Boston and the nation were riveted by the Sacco-Vanzetti case, which ended with their execution on August 22, 1927, and a new life as martyrs. Nicola Sacco and Bartolomeo Vanzetti were convicted of robbery and attendant murder in 1921. Their supporters challenged that verdict, arguing they were depicted as "radicals" and the evidence tainted to convict them on political grounds. When A. T. Fuller, governor of Massachusetts, denied them a second trial, public outcry demanded a review of the case. This photograph shows protesters—with a good sprinkling of uniformed police among them—circling the Common. (Courtesy *Boston Herald*.)

Beginning with rowdy demonstrations against the English Stamp Act and the tax on tea, the Common had become an accepted place of protest through the centuries. In October 1931, it drew the committed and the curious to the Communist Party strike rally on the Charles Street Mall. Very few women's heads show among the caps and fedoras. (Courtesy BPL, Leslie Jones Collection.)

In a climate of labor unrest, radical Edith Beckman spoke at another Communist Party rally on the Common that fall. She protested that the U.S. government wanted to deport her to Poland because she organized strikes. (Courtesy BPL, Leslie Jones Collection.)

If there was a favorite spot on the Common, it was the Frog Pond and still is. Here the yachting season lasted from April, when the basin was filled, to late fall, when this idyllic 1931 view was taken by *Globe* photographer Edmunds E. Bond. Making "pond boats," as they were called, was a favorite activity at summer camp or in seventh-grade shop class. The season started with

the Parks Department's contest for model boats of various types. One boy won with a Chinese junk. No matter the size, all the yachts sported jibs, but only a few young designers favored the gaff-rigged. There were races in the fall, and no one seemed to mind the wet feet sometimes involved in launching a boat. (Re-published with permission of the Globe Newspaper Company.)

A marble competition drew a ring of men and boys—and a few mothers—to the Common in 1924. It was sponsored by the *Herald Traveler* newspaper, which likely employed many entrants as paperboys. Here a referee observes from his stepladder (upper right), and an officer (left center) stands with his bugle behind him. (Courtesy BPL, Leslie Jones Collection.)

Girls competed at the Parks Department's annual hopscotch tournament. In May 1937, a group of 40 finalists from an original field of 1,600 met on the Common for the championship match. Mothers, fathers, and siblings look on as three contestants negotiate the regulation hopscotch grids painted on the concrete surface along the Tremont Street Mall. (Courtesy BPL.)

Since the Common was less than a mile from the warming ocean, sometimes the city had to provide snow for sledding. Kids in December 1930 had it both ways, with the real thing on the ground and more on the elevated wooden coast set up behind the Soldiers and Sailors Monument. Steps in the middle led to the top. (Courtesy BPL, Leslie Jones Collection.)

Photographer Leslie Jones often took photographs of Boston kids, like this young crowd mugging and waving from the Frog Pond around 1930. Surprisingly, this is our first image of children actually *in* the Frog Pond. Too shallow for swimming, it suits fine for splashing and wading. The fountain, once a spectacular 100-foot jet, is still a hit today. (Courtesy BPL, Leslie Jones Collection.)

Boston's tercentennial celebration in 1930 was a yearlong affair. Pictured here is a scene from July 4, when an audience gathered at twilight on the banks of the Frog Pond, "a natural amphitheater." Following reveille and lowering of the flag, there was a patriotic pageant under artificial lights. The gala year climaxed in September with a whole week of events, including the dedication of the Founders Monument. (Courtesy FPG.)

Hurricanes were not named in the days when "the Thirty-eight," as everyone called it, hit on September 21. While the wind snapped trees and limbs, as seen here on the Common, there had been weeks of rain that month, and the wind simply sucked many trees from the sodden earth. (Courtesy FPG.)

The trees have not leafed yet in 1927, when engine companies of the Boston Fire Department draw up on Tremont Street and point their hoses onto the Common for a high-pressure test. The tall rig shooting its spray was used to fight fires on high floors. This image gives a fine view of the new wings of the Massachusetts State House, added about 10 years earlier. (Courtesy BPL, Leslie Jones Collection.)

As late as 1939, the Boston Fire Department was still making annual appearances on the Common to show off its new techniques and equipment—a tradition that had started when hoses succeeded water buckets. In this photograph, a fireman jumps from a tall wooden tower into a rescue net below. A large crowd observes the action from a safe distance. (Courtesy Bostonian Society/Old State House.)

Once again the world went to war, and once again the Common became a training field for the military. In this 1940s photograph, soldiers bivouac on a muddy piece of ground that in happier days was laid out as ball fields. Note the stacked rifles in the center of this view. (Courtesy FPG.)

War bond rallies returned to the Common, as did victory parades to rally Bostonians, such as this June 1943 procession honoring crew members from the bomber Memphis Belle. Seated high on the backs of the jeeps are the heroes themselves. Note the boys on the lower right with GI-style crew cuts. (Courtesy BPL, Leslie Jones Collection.)

110

Labor strife was not unknown during the war years. In 1945, when a shortage of hogs caused the John P. Squires Company to curtail the workweek, members of Local 165 United Packinghouse Workers took to the Common to protest. "We are not on strike," they declared. "We want work to win the war." (Courtesy BPL, Leslie Jones Collection.)

With the gilt dome of the Massachusetts State House on the horizon, sailors and their girls keep company on benches along the Frog Pond. Note the little dog on the right end of the bench. Newspapers were fond of scenes of the Common in all weather, and press photographers found it easy work. (Courtesy BPL, Leslie Jones Collection.)

A photographer from the *Boston Herald* recorded this scene on the Common on the morning of August 15, 1945. It shows the aftermath of celebrations for the Japanese surrender the previous day. The war was over, and the cleanup would soon begin. The caption writer quipped, "Well, at least these fellers can't fall out of bed." (Courtesy BPL.)

Seven

"THE PEOPLE'S PARK"

The political unrest of the 1960s and 1970s made compelling news, and the press was always there to cover it. By the time George McGovern addressed an antiwar rally in 1969, the print and video cameras had become a big part of the occasion. The images in this chapter not only chronicle the events of these years but also reflect the emerging role of the media in "newsmaking."

On October 1, 1979, Pope John Paul II conducted Mass on the Common for an estimated 400,000 faithful. Despite heavy rains, crowds filled the Parade Ground and adjacent Flagstaff Hill. This aerial view shows the murky skies of the day, shrouding the tops of both Hancock towers. (Courtesy *Boston Herald*.)

On May 20, 1950, some 10,000 people dined on the Parade Ground. The *Herald* reported that almost 50,000 showed up, and the event was sold-out by noon. The menu included authentic Boston baked beans (five tons of them), potatoes, brown bread, Parker House rolls, and hot apple pie. Thousands of latecomers watched hungrily from the sidelines. (Courtesy Bostonian Society/Old State House.)

To this day, cows make a brief return at the annual Boston Common Dairy Festival, pictured here in 1951, with the new John Hancock building dominating the Back Bay skyline. Completed four years earlier, it is 26 stories high—Boston's first real skyscraper. Silhouetted against a cloudless sky, its signature weather beacon is surely signaling "clear blue, clear view." (Courtesy BPL.)

Sunday afternoon orators had held forth on the Common for more than a century, and the tradition was still alive in April 1950, when 31-year-old Billy Graham held an outdoor revival. It was a cold, wet day when some 50,000 people gathered to hear the fiery young evangelist. To warm spirits, the awaiting crowd was led in a sing-along of popular hymns and revivalist pieces. (Courtesy BPL.)

In the 1940s, the controversial Jesuit priest Leonard Feeney drew hundreds to the Common, where he declared salvation limited to Catholics. While this was established doctrine, Feeney made it into a rant against Jews and Protestants. Coming so soon after the Holocaust, this embarrassed the Vatican, which suppressed the view by suppressing Feeney. Expelled by the Jesuits in 1949, ex-communicated in 1952 but later reconciled, Feeney died in 1978. (Courtesy BPL.)

On October 22, 1952, presidential candidate Dwight D. Eisenhower spoke at a large campaign rally on the Parade Ground. Mamie Eisenhower sat behind him. Note the privileged position of the press corps, which includes both a couple of early television cameramen and a representative from Western Union. Hereafter almost every major political event would receive this kind of press coverage. (Courtesy BPL.)

Two weeks earlier, Eisenhower's running mate, Richard Nixon, had visited the Common. Here his motorcade moves through crowds along the Charles Street Mall. Pat Nixon sits beside him, and the Massachusetts junior senator Henry Cabot Lodge rides in the front seat. The Eisenhower-Nixon ticket took Massachusetts in November, but Lodge lost his Senate seat to John F. Kennedy. This shady path would soon disappear. (Courtesy BPL.)

A half-century after subway construction destroyed the Tremont Street Mall, the Charles Street Mall received similar treatment, as the City of Boston built a 1,300-car underground parking garage. In this 1959 aerial photograph, the entire Parade Ground has been scraped down and readied for excavation. Many of the trees along Charles Street still stand, though they, too, will ultimately be taken. (Courtesy Bostonian Society/Old State House.)

Seen from ground level in the autumn of 1960, the garage is about a year from completion. The horse-drawn wagons are gone, but the scene evokes the images of the previous century (see pages 77–79). Much of the work eventually proved to be faulty, and beginning in 1992, the garage was closed down for three years for repairs and reconstruction. (Courtesy BPL.)

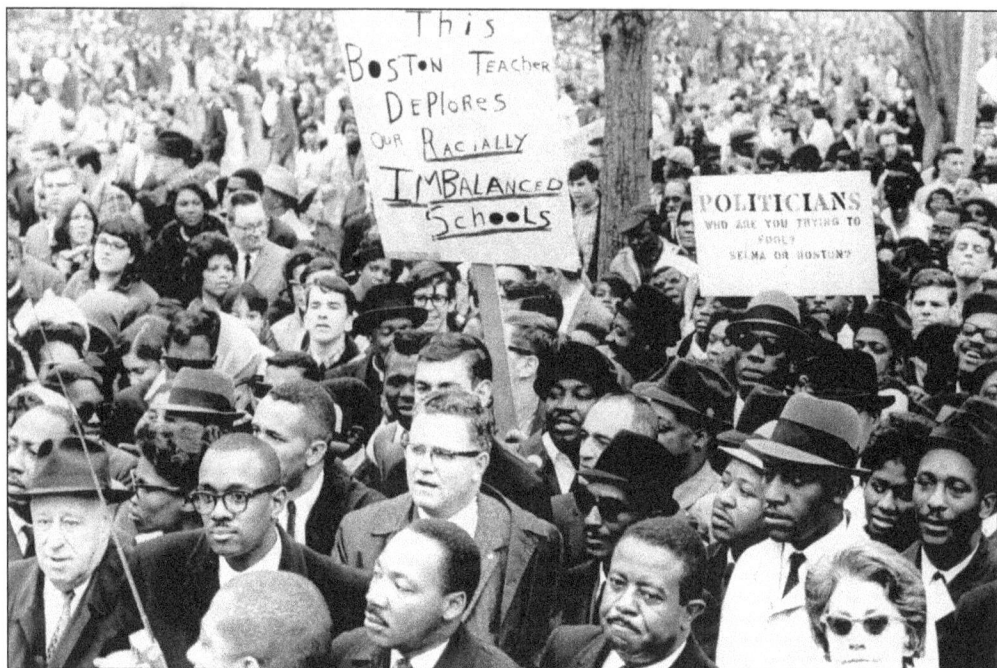

On April 23, 1965, Martin Luther King Jr. led a mile-long freedom march through the streets of Boston and onto the Common. Speaking from the Parkman Bandstand, King called for accelerated desegregation of housing and schools and for "destruction of the ghetto." After two hours of singing and speeches, the crowd dispersed in a steady rain, singing "We Shall Overcome." (Courtesy BPL.)

The Common became the epicenter of the so-called hippie invasion. Gathered at the Beacon-Charles corner in July 1968, these "flower children" seem unconcerned that they are attracting attention. (Courtesy *Boston Herald*.)

This photograph tells much about the course of news photography by October 1969, when George McGovern addressed some 100,000 at the Boston Common Vietnam Moratorium Rally. Behind a field of microphones, McGovern gives the victory sign to a throng of reporters, photographers, and television cameras. In the background is the new (1967) Tremont-on-Common, which brought high-rise living to Tremont Street. (Courtesy United Press International.)

Clenched fists mix with high spirits at an antiwar demonstration on May 5, 1971. Billed by its organizers as the "Spring Offensive," the event brought out some 25,000 young protesters—and hundreds of police and guardsmen. In the end, the affair was peaceful, with only one arrest. When the rally broke up in late afternoon, many remained on the Common for a rock concert and psychedelic light show. (Courtesy BPL.)

Backed by Bobby Cole's 26-piece orchestra and wearing "a dazzling sequin pajama suit," the legendary Judy Garland gave a free concert on the Common in August 1967. The event, sponsored by Knickerbocker Beer, drew an audience of 100,000 fans, "the largest live audience ever to see her perform," according to her agent. (Courtesy *Boston Herald*.)

Through much of the 1970s, the dance and chant of the Hare Krishnas were familiar parts of the daily bustle near the Park Street subway station. Here the performers break for lunch, apparently cooked on site and served on paper plates. Pedestrians take no notice of the scene. (Courtesy *Boston Herald*.)

The day the Pope came to town, October 1, 1979, he was welcomed at Logan Airport by First Lady Rosalyn Carter and Humberto Cardinal Medeiros. After a 14-mile motorcade through the Boston neighborhoods, the Pope arrived at the Common, where 400,000 people were waiting in the rain. From a specially constructed podium, he then conducted the first papal Mass in North America. (Courtesy FPG.)

Michael Dukakis came to the Common on April 29, 1987, to formally declare his candidacy for the Democratic nomination for president. Here he acknowledges the support of the assembled crowd as his wife, Kitty, smiles proudly beside him. Though Governor Dukakis lost the election to George H. W. Bush, he carried Massachusetts with 54 percent of the vote. (Courtesy Boston Herald.)

Seiji Ozawa's quarter-century as music director of the Boston Symphony Orchestra was celebrated with a free concert on the Common on Sunday afternoon, September 25, 1999, before a crowd of 80,000. Ozawa, sick with the flu, appeared on stage to conduct the final movement of Beethoven's Ninth Symphony. The *Globe* music critic called his performance "vigorous, well shaped, and awesomely intense." (Photograph by Michael Lutch; courtesy Boston Symphony Orchestra.)

The centennial of Saint-Gaudens's Shaw Memorial was celebrated on May 30, 1997. Ceremonies included a reenactment of the 1897 parade and an address by Colin Powell, retired chairman of the Joint Chiefs of Staff. (Courtesy *Boston Herald*.)

Eight

THE FIFTH CENTURY

Considering the few short years since the millennium celebrations, recent events on the Common can hardly be viewed as history. Thus these last several pages take the form of a small album of snapshots of the Common as it enters its fifth century. They also serve as a reminder that though the Common changes with the times, certain pictorial themes recur through the years.

Since 1700, when the new year was welcomed with a blast of trumpets on the Common, Bostonians have returned to mark the beginning of each subsequent century. To celebrate the millennium, there was First Night, an annual citywide event, attended by one million revelers. Again the Common served as a focal point with presentations and fireworks and ice sculptures at the Frog Pond. With warm temperatures on December 31, 1999, the sculptures in the foreground show signs of melting as others are hoisted into place. (Photograph by Barbara W. Moore.)

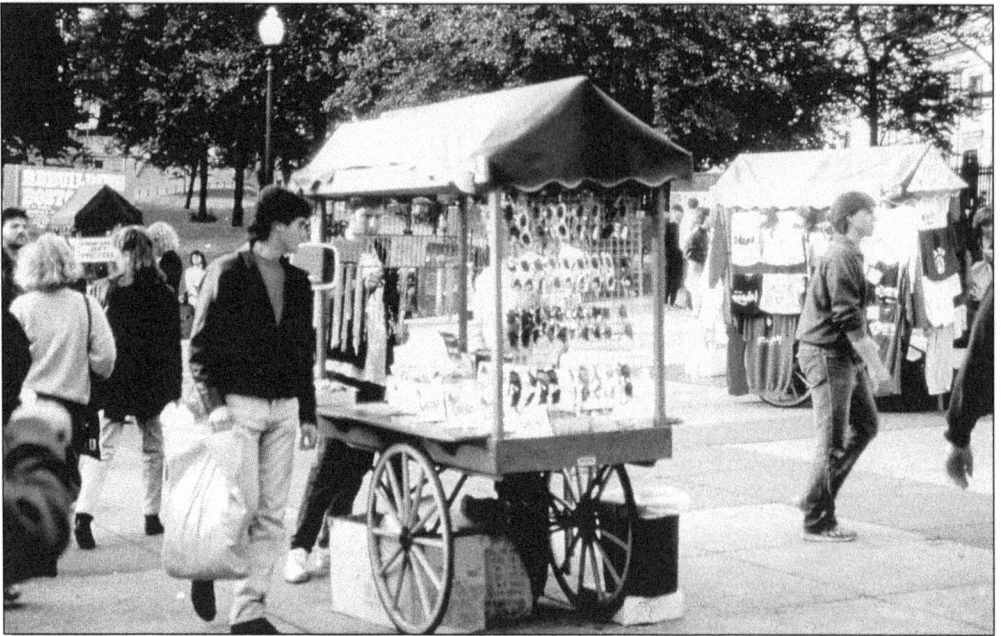

Although a far cry from "Apple Mary," vendors still ply their wares on the Common today. Now limited to 35 specified sites, many purvey food and (nonalcoholic) drink. Others, like those seen above, offer a variety of souvenirs. (Photograph by Henry Lee.)

In the 19th-century tradition of park keepers, the Park Rangers serve on horse and on foot as interpreters, guides, and guardians of the city's principal parks. Formed in 1983 with private funding, the group has become a valued arm of the Parks Department. Here a ranger assists a visitor in front of the new Boston Common Information Center. (Courtesy Boston Parks and Recreation Department.)

124

In the 18th and 19th centuries, Native American visitors drew large and interested crowds to the Common. Each May since 2002, members of the Wampanog Nation have joined in celebrating the Ancient Fishweir Project, a student-built replica of the 5,000-year-old fishweirs discovered during excavation of the subway beneath Boylston Street. (Photograph by Henry Lee.)

The Ancient and Honorable Artillery Company, formed in 1638, still elects its officers and performs annual military drills on the Common, a reminder of the long history of both the company and the grounds. This annual event is the most direct link with the 17th-century Common. (Photograph by Barbara W. Moore.)

After years of disuse, the Frog Pond has been renewed once again as an artificial ice-skating rink in winter and a spray and wading pool in summer. Operated by the Frog Pond Foundation, it attracts more than 100,000 winter skaters, and almost as many children enjoy the wading pool each summer. (Courtesy Boston Parks and Recreation Department.)

The Common has always been a resort for children, and its slopes and fields still provide open space for coasting and organized sports. Even so, there was no children's playground until about 1950. In 2002, this facility was renewed through private benefaction as the Tadpole Totlot, providing a happy respite for child and mother alike. (Courtesy Boston Parks and Recreation Department.)

As shown in Christian Remick's depiction of 1768 (see page 18), dogs have long been a part of Common life, though limited in the 18th century to 14 inches in height to prevent the biting of cow udders. With size no longer a problem, dogs and their owners now gather to socialize in designated space by the Parade Ground. (Photograph by Eugenie Beal.)

The Parkman Bandstand, which has served as a rostrum for orators like James Michael Curley and Martin Luther King Jr., may be unsuited for today's mass events. But it provides an ideal site for smaller-scale activities such as midday band concerts, Shakespearean productions, and children's theater. (Courtesy Boston Parks and Recreation Department.)

As always, there is sledding. The double ripper of yesteryear has given way to the plastic saucer, but after every fresh, new snowfall, neighborhood children still come to Flagstaff Hill for the best coasting in town. (Photograph by Henry Lee.)

128

www.ingramcontent.com/pod-product-compliance
Lightning Source LLC
Chambersburg PA
CBHW080601110426
42813CB00006B/1367